Jenny Wilson was born in England in 1959. Her parents came to live in Adelaide when Jenny was 6 months of age. After completing her schooling Jenny studied Maths and Music at the University of Adelaide before completing a Diploma of Education. She taught Maths for fifteen years at schools in Adelaide and in England. Jenny left teaching to embark on a Bachelor of Theology. She was ordained a Deacon and Priest in 2006. Jenny is currently Associate Priest and Precentor at St Peter's Cathedral in Adelaide.

ABOUT
Life

A selection of Jenny Wilson's sermons
from St Peter's Anglican Cathedral

St Peter's
nurturing spirit and mind
CATHEDRAL

St Peter's Cathedral
27 King William Street
North Adelaide
South Australia 5006

First published 2011

Editorial team: Angela Evans, Nick Iles, Di Nichols, Sue Stack, Kathy Teague

Published in association with Wakefield Press
Front cover photograph by Mick Bradley
Tile photographs by Leonard D. Long
Designed and typeset by Liz Nicholson, designBITE
Printed and bound by Hyde Park Press

ISBN 978 1 74305 024 8

CONTENTS

INTRODUCTION

Life is complex and varied, difficult and delightful, challenging and rewarding. In this series of short reflections Jenny Wilson tackles some of its deep questions, taking us on a journey with her from early morning bird watching to the hospitality of God, from suffering to the anchoring role of story in our lives. Thought-provoking, poetic and grounded in everyday experience, these contemporary observations encourage us to see God in new ways, stripped of devotional religiosity. Here we are encouraged to join Jenny on a deeply personal, intimate journey with the God who is both mysterious and yet present through all the shades of life.

The Very Rev'd Dr Sarah Macneil
Dean (2009–2011)

'SIR, WE WISH TO SEE JESUS.'

When my oldest friend and I were at university, my friend was studying bird life in biology and one of her assignments involved watching a variety of species of birds at the Mouth of the River Murray. We set our alarms at 4:30 am, ate breakfast bleary-eyed, drank, in my case I am sure several quick cups of tea and set off in the brown mini in which I learnt to drive. We were staying at our family beach house near Port Elliot, our bird watching destination was the Murray Mouth. Our task to be what the writer of today's psalm called 'watchers for the morning'.[1]

My soul looks for the Lord, the psalmist writes,
More than watchers for the morning
More I say than watchers for the morning.

Our watch was for birds as the morning appeared but keeping watch for anything of beauty has woven into it, I think, a keeping watch for God.

It was the first time I had gone bird watching and I didn't forget it. I love birds, the sound of them, the flight of them, the pottering way they hunt for food. This love was born that day, watching for

---

1   Psalm 130: 5, 6

birds near the mouth of the river, a river that is now struggling for life, gasping for breath.

What is the watch we keep there now? I'm scared for it. Worried about this place where one of my great loves was born. Scared for the home of the birds I so enjoy. I'm worried about the River Murray. Where's God in this?

Some Greeks went up to worship at the festival. They came to Philip who was from Bethsaida in Galilee and said to him, 'Sir, we wish to see Jesus.' [2]

Sir, we wish to see Jesus. Wherever we are, in whatever situation we find ourselves, this is our desire; the longing of those who keep watch, by a struggling river, by the bedside of a dearly loved friend, in the midst of our Anglican church floundering in its struggle for unity, or those coming to the festival in Jerusalem two thousand years ago.

Sir, we wish to see Jesus.

The Greeks who asked for Jesus had come to Jerusalem at the feast of the Passover and they must have heard of his arrival. Just prior to our gospel passage is John's account of Jesus' triumphal entry into Jerusalem on a young donkey. The writer comments, quoting the prophet Zechariah, 'Do not be afraid, daughter of Zion. Look, your king is coming sitting on a donkey's colt.' [3] The crowd might well be puzzled, if not afraid. The signs are that Jesus is not behaving as the warrior king for whom they had hoped. Look, the prophet said, keep watch, keep watch for the one who embodies the kingdom of God.

2   John 12:20
3   John 12:15

Sir, we wish to see Jesus.

Andrew and Philip went and told Jesus, and the one who entered Jerusalem on a donkey's colt spoke with them. 'The hour has come . . . Very truly I tell you, unless a grain of wheat falls into the earth and dies, it remains just a single grain; but if it dies, it bears much fruit. Those who love their life will lose it but those who hate their life in this world will keep it for eternal life. Whoever serves me must follow me, and where I am there will my servant be also.'[4]

Sir, we wish to see Jesus.

What those Greeks were given were strange truths. The truth of the reign of God. The truth of what it is to live as one who follows Jesus. Jesus paints before our searching eyes the image of a grain broken and dying in the earth and bids us see our lives that way. If you cling to life you will lose it, if you hate it, or, we might say, if you hold it lightly, you will keep it for eternal life. And then the promise of Jesus' abiding presence. Where I am, there will my servant be also.

Sir, we wish to see Jesus.

And what we find is one who invites us to give up our life that we might strangely gain it, to be broken that we and creation might strangely thrive. And what we find is one who promises his abiding presence.

My soul looks for the Lord,
More than watchers for the morning
More I say than watchers for the morning.

Those who keep watch give up something of their life. Those who seek Jesus allow a letting go of their life. Those who wait, not quite knowing for what it is that they are waiting, allow a brokenness.

---

4   John 12:23–26

Broken in them is the need to control, the need to take charge of life. Those who keep watch, those who seek Jesus embark on the way of faith. The walk of faith involves holding lightly onto life.

I'm worried about the River Murray. I listen to the news straining for solutions. If only six properties up river were purchased, the lower lakes would be saved. If only the government would regulate the demands of irrigators, the river would revive. If only we would accept that some crops were not meant to be grown here . . . If only it would rain some more . . . If only . . .

Whilst there is a time and a place for radios and action, for fighting for practical solutions, there is also a time to keep watch. To abandon for a little while the need to take control, and to sit waiting to hear the voice of God. To be watchers in the morning. In the place of our concern, be it our friend or our church or our river that is struggling to thrive, to whisper, 'Sir, we wish to see Jesus.'

And to remember that the one we seek will ask us to sit lightly with our life. That the one for whom we keep watch will bid us to allow our need to take control to be broken. That the one who embodies God's kingdom will promise us his abiding presence in any place where hope seems to be lost.

Quite a number of years ago now my oldest friend and I kept watch for birds as morning broke near the mouth of the River Murray. We were watchers in the morning.

 Sermon for Evensong Sunday 7 September 2008

WE ARE
NOT ALONE

The theology of the Hebrew Scriptures was fairly clear about the issue of suffering. If you obeyed God, things went well with you. If you disobeyed God, and, in particular, if you worshipped other gods, things would not go so well. However, the wisdom writer of the Book of Job sought to challenge this theology. His book opens with a description of a man called Job, a man who was 'blameless and upright, who feared God and turned away from evil'.[1] Things were going well with Job.

In the heavenly places, a mythical character, the Satan, challenges God about Job. The word Satan literally means the *accuser*. The Satan, the Accuser, puts his accusation to God. He suspects Job's motivation. Job is only loyal to God in order that things will continue to go well for him. The Accuser challenges God, asking God to allow him to revoke Job's good fortune, to test Job's loyalty. God agrees.

Even after the loss of family and possessions, Job blesses God in his grief. With God's permission, the Accuser strikes again. Job is covered with a skin disease which 'inflicted loathsome sores on Job from the sole of his foot to the crown of his head'.[2] Job sits amidst

---

1   Job 1:1
2   Job 2:7

some ashes, saying to his wife, 'Shall we receive the good at the hand of God and not receive the bad?'[3] Even in the midst of such suffering, Job maintains his loyalty. Job will not curse God.

Before we look at what happens next, we need to reflect a little on the mythical figure of the Accuser. The Accuser does not believe in the relationship between God and a human being. He does not believe that the relationship between God and a human being can survive in any situation but success. The Accuser accuses Job – and all humanity – of being fair weather friends. Such a relationship cannot withstand the onset of suffering and so, of course, such a relationship is worthless. That is the Accuser's challenge to God. That no human being can continue in relationship with God in suffering, that human beings only relate to God for what God will give them.

Firstly, though, the writer of Job explores Job's relationships with his friends. Job, covered with sores, sits in his ash heap and three of his friends enter the scene. Job's friends, Eliphaz, Bildad and Zophar have heard of his troubles. They meet together to go and console and comfort him. At the sight of Job, their distress is acute – they weep aloud, tear their robes and throw dust upon their heads. And they sit with him on the ground for seven days and seven nights and for that time they sit in silence.[4] Not bad pastoral care really. These friends do a pretty good job of keeping Job company in his place of struggle. Until, that is, Job begins to speak.

For after this seven days of silence, the book of Job contains a series of dialogues between Job and his three friends. Job, overwhelmed by his suffering laments his birth. Once Eliphaz, Bildad and Zophar begin to respond, they cannot resist the

---

3   Job 2:10
4   Job 2:12–13

theology of their culture. They present the doctrine of rewards and punishments. His friends point out, in the helpful way that friends often do, that Job must have committed some sin for which his suffering is the punishment. 'If iniquity is in your hand, put it far away,' they advise.[5] Job protests that he has committed no sin that could be responsible for such suffering. He calls his friends 'miserable comforters'[6] and speakers of 'windy words'.[7] The friends who kept company with Job for a time, now desert him. They do not listen to his truth. They cannot believe that he is not to blame for his suffering. To accept the fact that suffering might just be inflicted upon us is too confronting for them. And so they desert him, as friends often do, by being deaf to his reality, by silencing him with their 'windy words'. The relationship between Job and his friends has failed. The Accuser would be smiling in the wings. So far, he is vindicated. Human relationships, at least, do not seem to be able to withstand the suffering of the innocent.

But, what of the relationship between Job and God?

Job bewails the absence of God in his suffering. God has deserted Job – 'if I go forward, he is not there,' Job cries, 'or backward, I cannot perceive him . . .'[8] Job begs God for vindication, for the opportunity to 'lay [his] case before him'.[9] Finally, Job cries out, 'let the Almighty answer me!'[10] Job longs for God's presence, for an encounter with God. It is as if Job wants to take God to court! To challenge the theology that says his suffering is punishment for sin, for he knows of no sin worthy of this punishment.

In the final chapters of the Book of Job, God answers Job. God

---

5   Job 11:14
6   Job 16:2
7   Job 16:3
8   Job 23:8
9   Job 23:4
10 Job 31:35

answers Job 'out of a whirlwind.'[11] And, as God answers Job, God answers the Accuser as well.

God does not explain anything. God does not even engage with Job's questions. Instead God bombards Job with question upon question, encounter upon encounter, leading Job to contemplate the mystery of creation. 'Where were you when I laid the foundation of the earth? Tell me if you have understanding. Who determined its measurements – surely you know! Or who stretched the line upon it? On what were its bases sunk, or who laid its cornerstone when the morning stars sang together and all the heavenly beings shouted for joy.'[12] Question upon question, encounter upon encounter, through four chapters, God barely draws breath, as God wrestles Job from his world view fraught with darkness and despair to a glimpse of God's vision.

When God is finally silent, Job replies: 'I know that you can do all things and that no purpose of yours can be thwarted . . . Hear and I will speak; I will question you, and you declare to me. I have heard of you by the hearing of the ear, but now my eye sees you'.[13]

What God gives Job is not an explanation but an encounter. The suffering of the innocent Job is not made comprehensible in any of God and Job's wrestling but we see what God gives. God gives God's presence as Job gave Job's presence, remaining true to himself. Job poured out his truth to his God and God honoured that outpouring. The Accuser got it wrong. In the midst of suffering we see the relationship between Creator and the created one thriving. In the midst of acute suffering, Job experienced an encounter with God which transformed his relationship with God and transformed his life.

---

11   Job 38:1
12   Job 38:4–7
13   Job 42:2, 4–6

Not all of us find ourselves on ash heaps like Job's. But some of us do. Some of us find that we have taken away from us livelihood and possessions, or our good health, or a loved one too precious to lose. The wisdom writer of the Book of Job speaks into our situation. The writer does not attempt to explain anything. Rather, the writer hints at the company in which we might find ourselves. He says two things. Firstly he says that those who love us will find it almost too difficult to accompany us without trying to look for an explanation about why we find ourselves suffering as we do. It is a rare friend who can just sit beside our ash heap. Secondly the writer speaks of God. And what he seems to be saying is this. If we can find the courage and the vulnerability and the grace to pour out to God the truth of our suffering, then we may sense that we are not alone.

 Sermon for Evensong Sunday 4 October 2009

GOD'S HOSPITALITY

It might be tempting to believe that all scripture is written by the hand of God. In fact scripture is written by human hands and it is read by human eyes. The hands that wrote scripture had a context in which they lived and a purpose for which they wrote. The eyes that read scripture equally have a context in which they live and a purpose for which they read. We read scripture through the lens of our life. Biblical scholars look at scripture through different lenses and their insights can enliven our own. One such scholar, Brendon Byrne, a Jesuit who works in Victoria, has explored Luke's gospel through the lens of *hospitality*. His book is called *The Hospitality of God*.[1] In memory of Saint Luke, we will spend a little time with his ideas.

Luke sees the life and ministry of Jesus as a visitation of God to Israel and the world. As the gospel unfolds we witness characters being given the opportunity to offer hospitality to this visitor, Jesus, and we watch bystanders respond and comment. It would be difficult to read Luke's gospel without noticing that a lot of meals take place. In this we see also Jesus offering hospitality, often in unexpected places, and again, we are given glimpses of the response of those keeping watch on his behaviour. Luke is fascinated by the

---

1   Byrne, Brendon, *The Hospitality of God: A Reading of Luke's Gospel,* Australian edition published by St Paul's Publications, Strathfield, 2000

human response to Jesus' presence and activity. Jesus brings healing and life. One might expect that he would be met with the embrace of a hungry and broken people. As we know well, this is not always the case.

One of the first characters to encounter the opportunity to offer God hospitality is, of course, Mary. Her first offer of hospitality though is to Gabriel. Angels are messengers and Gabriel's message, Gabriel's invitation to Mary to offer hospitality to God's child in her womb, shakes her to the core of her being. 'How can this be?'[2] Welcoming God as a visitor is rarely a comfortable experience. Mary senses the depth of God's request. She offers the hospitality the angel requests – 'Here I am', she says, 'Let it be with me according to your word.'[3] Mary's response is an icon of the welcome for which God longs.

Jesus' visits often occur in unexpected places. He is nurtured in the womb of a young woman in a remote region of Galilee. And towards the end of Luke's gospel, he invites himself to stay at the home of Zacchaeus, a rich tax collector. Zacchaeus is not himself at home in Jericho where he resides. He would have been excluded from the society of those around him because of his work as a tax collector. But it is with an excluded one with whom Jesus seeks hospitality. Zacchaeus is brought to life by his encounter with Jesus 'Today salvation has come to this house,'[4] Jesus comments, 'the Son of Man has come to seek out and save the lost.'[5] The citizens of Jericho, however, were not impressed with Jesus' choice of residence – they grumbled, 'He has gone to be the guest of one who is a sinner.'[6]

2   Luke 1:34
3   Luke 1:38
4   Luke 19:9
5   Luke 19:10
6   Luke 19:6

This is not the only place that grumbling occurs in Luke's gospel. Jesus' choice of dinner companions often invites comment and in Chapter 15 the religious authorities have reason to protest. 'This fellow welcomes sinners and eats with them',[7] the Pharisees and the scribes complain. Jesus responds to them with one of the most beautiful and revealing set of parables about the nature of God to be found in the gospel. Jesus tells three parables of the lost which culminate in the parable of the two sons. One can be in no doubt about God's response to sinners when we read of the father of the prodigal son running to greet him and of that same father counselling with compassion his jealous brother. Each of the parables portrays God as behaving with almost foolish exuberance as the God-character seeks out the coin or the sheep or the sons that have strayed. Luke's interest though is not just in the character of God. How do the bystanders respond? The first two parables point to the possibility of a joyous response to God's hospitality to God's lost one. Another all too human response, illustrated by the religious authorities, is possible too – that of grumbling. The parable of the two sons leaves these possible responses up in the air – we are not told if the older brother joins the banquet given to welcome home his prodigal brother. The text challenges us to consider our own response. As Brendon Bryne asks, 'Are we comfortable with the God who acts with the foolishness of love displayed by the characters in these parables?'[8] Can we offer hospitality to God whose own hospitality is so all embracing?

The people of the time, no different from our own, we might suspect, could not. Hospitality was, in the end, denied. So challenging was Jesus' presence that permission for his visit to

7   Luke 15
8   Byrne, Brendon, *The Hospitality of God*

continue was denied. And they crucified him to ensure that he did not stay with them any longer.

Walking along the Road to Emmaus, a few days later, two of Jesus' disciples try to make sense of what has happened. They find themselves in company with one who asks them, 'What are you discussing with each other while you are walking along?'[9] Their heavy response reveals their unhappiness. 'Are you the only visitor to Jerusalem who does not know the things that have happened in these days?'[10] Cleopas says. The irony of this question is unmistakable – the *only* visitor to Jerusalem who does not know what has happened there is in fact the divine visitor who was at the centre of the action.

Jesus walks with them, though they do not know it is him. And he hears their story, the story of hope shattered. And he puts their story in the context of the story of the scriptures, bridging the gap between what they had expected and what had actually happened; 'beginning with Moses and the prophets, he interpreted to them the things about himself in all the scriptures.'[11] And their hearts burnt within them as their lost hope was rekindled.

And then they shared another meal. They urged the strange visitor, this hope bearer, to stay with them; they didn't want him to go. Offered him hospitality not yet knowing that it was his hospitality that was about to be offered to them. As was the pattern through all Luke's gospel, the guest became host. And at the table, took bread, blessed and broke it. And then they knew. They knew it was the visitor that the world had failed to make welcome. And that God had broken the bounds of their rejection and had risen to invite them yet again into his life-giving embrace.

9   Luke 24:17
10   Luke 24:18
11   Luke 24:27

God's hospitality. God is always inviting us into God's life, where there's thriving to be had. Our circumstances may be similar to those found in a story in Luke's gospel. We may, like Mary, be chosen by God to bear, in some way, God's hope for the world. We may, like Zacchaeus, be unpopular in the world, but be chosen by God to offer hospitality to God in some human way. We may witness God's embrace of the lost and struggle to rejoice at God's abundant generosity as was the experience of the brother of the prodigal son. We may find ourselves walking along a road, not unlike the Emmaus road, wondering about a situation that seemed full of hope and in which we now find ourselves overwhelmed by loss. Wherever we are, that stranger is on the road trudging along beside us, that stranger who will place alongside our story the stories of God, and who will offer us hospitality in the rich life of God.

 Sermon for Evensong Sunday 19 October 2008

I WILL BRING YOU HOME

Tonight we hear a little snippet of a *story*.

The Lord said to Abram, after Lot had separated from him, 'Raise your eyes now, and look from the place where you are, northwards and southwards and eastwards and westwards; for all the land that you see I will give to you and to your offspring for ever. I will make your offspring like the dust of the earth . . .'[1]

Our Old Testament reading from the 13th chapter of the Book of Genesis tells of the arrival of Abram at the land which God has chosen for him to inhabit. In the previous chapter in the opening verses we find Abram going about his business. He is unconscious of the encounter and the request that is about to be made of him. Abram and his family are settled at Haran. His father Terah has died there. And then Abram has a visitor. He is addressed by the Lord. And the Lord is in an instructive mood.

'Go from your country and your kindred and your father's house to the land that I will show you,' says the Lord to Abram, 'I will make of you a great nation and I will bless you, and make your name great, so that you will be a blessing . . . and in you all the families of the earth shall be blessed.'[2]

---

1   Genesis 13:14–16
2   Genesis 12:1–3

Abram is abruptly addressed by God. And God's request is simply that he leave all that he knows and trust himself into the guidance of God. He is to leave all that is secure. 'Go from your country,' says God. Abram is to leave the land that is his home and his livelihood. 'Go from your kindred', your distant relatives. 'Go from your father's house', from your immediate family. Leave every layer of familiarity and structure that upholds your life, says God. In our world, we often see people make this kind of a move. Old Testament Scholars caution us, though, that, when we read of Abram's response to God, we must 'always remember that to leave home and to break ancestral bonds was to expect of ancient men almost the impossible'.[3] Of Abram, in Abram's time and place, God was demanding extraordinary trust. But trust Abram did. 'So Abram went', the text tells us.

In asking Abram to leave his country and his kindred and his father's house, God makes to Abram a significant promise. The encounter between them is made up of instruction and promise on God's part and then unquestioning trust on the part of Abram. God promises land, a land in which he can thrive, and God promises family. God promises that, of Abram, he will make a great nation, that the land that God will give him will be peopled by his family.

The promise of God, though, goes further than this. God promises that in Abram *all* the families of the earth shall be blessed. An extraordinary promise, this, that Abram's family will be a source of blessing for all people.

So Abram went.

And Abram, who God named Abraham when he made a covenant with him when he was ninety-nine years old, became the model of

3 Gerhard von Rad, *Genesis*, SCM Press Ltd Bloomsbury Street London (a translation 1961, 1972) p161

faith. Abraham became the one who showed exemplary trust in God. And in our reading tonight, we hear the story of his seeing the land that God has promised – of God's promise being fulfilled.

The story of Abraham, the stories of the patriarchs of Israel, make up part of the first five books of the Bible, known as the Torah. Stories were told orally, passed on from parents to children by the telling in community, until at a particular time in the history of the Israelite people, these stories were written down and organised into the form with which we are familiar.

I want to think about when they were written down, about the circumstances in which they were written down, and the need that was fulfilled in their writing.

The Torah reached its final form at the time of the exile. In the middle of the 6th century BC, a significant number of the Jewish community were deported by the Babylonians from Judah to Babylon.

The Israelite people in exile were a people without place, without land, without city, without temple, without king, a people who cried out as in the psalm,

'How shall we sing the Lord's song in a strange land?'[4]

Their struggle was profound.

And this resourceless people found they had just one resource. This displaced people found they had one place. And the resource, the place, . . . was *story*. When their land was far away and their place of worship was decimated, they found one thing to remind and uphold them in the identity that was their life . . . *story*. They told their *story*.

The Torah, what was written down of the different strands of the oral tradition of the people of Israel, is made up of two key types of writing, narrative and instruction – stories of the patriarchs and

---

4   Psalm 137:4

their encounters with God, and the commandments and laws that God gave the people through Moses. Laws that were guidance really, guidance from God about how the people with whom God lived in covenant relationship were to live their lives. Story and guidance woven together made up the Torah, the Torah that sustained the people when everything else was stripped away from them.

And what was one of the key narratives in this story, the story that sustained a people exiled from their home? The tale of a man, Abram, who was asked by God to willingly walk away from his home, from his people, from all that sustained him. The story of a man who was promised by God that he would be given land and offspring, as many as the stars in the heavens. The story of a man who was told by God that he was to 'raise his eyes' and see the land that God was to give him. That was the story that sustained those who were so far from home.

Many of us have times when all that sustains us is stripped away. When we are profoundly dislocated from all that seems to remind us of who we are. And dislocation is not always geographical. We can find ourselves exiled from our homes, from our sense of who we are, by illness, by grief, by disappointment. Many of the ordinary experiences of a human life leave us in exile.

Whatever it is that leaves us resourceless, displaced, homeless, we can find that there is one resource, one place, one home that remains. *Story*. Like the Israelite people in exile, we have *story* – the story of God and God's ways with God's people. The story of the God who lead Abram to the place where he could hear God say, 'raise your eyes and look where you are', the story of God who says to each one of us, 'I will bring you home'.

 Sermon for Evensong Sunday 7 February 2010

A TASTE
OF LIFE

There were seven cases of choir robes. Each case contained the cassock and surplice and ruffs and medals for five or six of the choristers who travelled on our choir's tour to England and Rome. Each case was named after a composer – Bruckner, Palestrina, Howells and so on – and one chorister was deemed the 'case captain' for each case. Before each service, every chorister would go to their case captain to collect their robes, and after each service, to the case captain, their robes would be returned. Those robes travelled on the bus that carried the choir all around England, sometimes the robes were in their cases, but more often they were wrapped in their groups in black plastic garbage bags. The bags hung right near the back of the bus. And the choristers who sat at the back of the bus – the trebles usually – were said to be going to Narnia, as it was just as if they were pushing their way through a wardrobe, full of choir robes, to get there.

'You are the salt of the earth',[1] Jesus said to his disciples, standing on a mountain at the beginning of his ministry in Galilee, encouraging them to maintain the essence of who they were, to

---

1   Matthew 5:13 You are the salt of the earth; but if salt has lost its taste, how can its saltiness be restored? It is no longer good for anything, but is thrown out and trampled under foot.

inspire those around them. What he didn't say, was how much work it would take . . .

There were six boxes of music. The choir sang Evensong in seven English Cathedrals, at the Eucharist in England and Rome, wonderfully at St Peter's Basilica, as well as at two concerts. Each night before the choir was to sing, a small group gathered to organize the music. Each chorister had a black folder that they used for services and plastic folder in which their music was stored. The small group would remove music from the previous service and place, in the black folder, the music for the next service. Night after night, before each service, this band of music librarians beavered away.

'Let your light shine before others',[2] Jesus said. What he didn't say, was that there may be hours, days, years of preparation for every moment when that light shines.

The Choir Tour was in the planning for more than eighteen months. A group met early in the year 2009 and the emails began. Choristers and parents and the Director of Music embarked on the task of negotiating with Cathedrals and Churches where the choir might sing, hotels in which the choir and their tag-a-long team of parents and partners might stay, restaurants for meals and of course flights to get us there and buses to transport us when we had arrived. There were 56 of us in the main group, and many other parents and people who knew the choir and the Cathedral community came close to the tour for pieces of time.

'Let your light shine before others', Jesus said. Never letting on as he said it, just how much work it would be. When he talked

---

2   Matthew 5:14–16 You are the light of the world . . . No one after lighting a lamp puts it under the bushel basket, but on the lamp-stand, and it gives light to all in the house. Jesus said. In the same way, let your light shine before others, so that they may see your good works and give glory to your Father in heaven.

about bushels and lamp-stands, one might have imagined that it was simply a matter of having the courage to step out from under that bushel, blinking in the sun that helps us shine. And courage is often a significant part of what it takes. But often too so is hard work, and work over such a long period of time.

I guess if we reflect on the source of our light's human life we would have realized. We would have realized that to shine in a way that brings glory to God sometimes needs years of work and struggle. Jesus, after all, faced the rejection of those near to him and confrontation with the leaders of the faith that was the source of his life. He faced terror and torture and a shameful death before God revealed through him the light that shone beyond his death in the resurrection. We might have known, if we reflected on Jesus' life, that stepping out from under a bushel to let our light shine before others would not be easy.

'Let your light shine before others', Jesus said. And our choir did shine. They sang Howells canticles at Peterborough and Canterbury Cathedrals, they sang the Darke in F mass setting at a Eucharist in Wells in Somerset, they sang anthems by Vaughan Williams and Walton as midnight struck on New Year's Eve at the Watchnight service in Salisbury, and they sang Palestrina's *Missa Brevis* at the Papal Basilicas of Santa Maria Maggiore and St Peter at the Vatican in Rome. And their music was woven with the beautiful organ playing of Josh who was an organ scholar and chorister here a number of years ago.

We are not all singers or members of a choir. And the way in which we are to shine is different for each one of us and at different times of our lives. For the people of Queensland facing the aftermath of cyclone as well as the devastating floods of a few weeks ago, one might wonder what it is to be salt and light in such circumstances and what extraordinary courage and determination it might take. For members of a Cathedral community like ours, we are each called to be light at the time and place in which we find ourselves. In the ordinary times. When we are working, raising children, facing the joy and struggle of getting older. In light times, when life seems to have a gentle tread, and in darker times when we walk the path of a grief that we know will never leave us and in which we wonder if we can possibly imagine shining and giving glory to God. Jesus' words on that mountain are surely for us all and for each moment of our lives.

During the tour on which our choir travelled to England and Rome, they did sing in a number of cathedrals and churches. And they sang in other places as well. They sang a version of Waltzing Mathilda – 'Time for a Matilda', Mrs Hempton would say – in Adelaide Airport before they flew out, in the Angel Spice, an Indian Restaurant near Peterborough to the delight of the restaurant's owner Jack, and in the Square in front of St Peter's Basilica in Rome. And they also sang what is really their party piece, 'Locus iste' by Bruckner. The words of 'Locus iste', roughly translated, mean 'this is the place'. And the choir sang 'Locus iste' underground in the catacombs near Rome in the company of the Australian Salesian priest who gave a tour there.

But they sang 'Locus iste' somewhere else as well. On New Years' Day, a tired choir, who had sung the Watch-night Service at the Cathedral in Salisbury the night before, found themselves on the bus being driven to see the sights in the county of Wiltshire near Salisbury. After paying homage to Stonehenge, the bus drove the group to Old Sarum, a site of some ancient ruins high up on a hill. I stood away from the group looking at the view for a while. As I turned around, I noticed that the choir was gathering around

Leonie, almost by instinct, it seemed. And there, on a hill in Wiltshire, the choir sang '*Locus iste*', by Anton Bruckner, and there in that place, as in many others during their tour of England and Rome, they shone and gave glory to their father who is in heaven.

 Sermon for Eucharist Sunday 6 February 2011